TEN THOUSAND CHILDREN

True stories told by children who escaped
the Holocaust on the Kindertransport

This book is dedicated to the 1.5 million children who perished in the Holocaust.

We wish to thank the late Dr. Nora Levin who originated the Oral History Archives at Gratz College, Philadelphia, and the many *Kinder* who contributed their stories and photographs.

The publisher gratefully acknowledges the cooperation of the following sources of photographs for this book: The Berlin Museum: 57; Bildarchiv Preussischer Kulturbesitz: 32; Anne L. Fox and Eva Abraham-Podietz and other kinder: 14, 19, 21, 22, 25, 31, 34, 39, 41, 43, 45, 46, 47, 48, 49, 50, 52, 55, 56, 69, 70, 71, 75, 79, 83, 84, 86, 91, 94, 95, 96, 97, 98, 103 (top), 104, 109, 111, 114, 115, 116, 117, 119, 121, 127; Collection of Walter Karliner, courtesy of Museum of Jewish Heritage, New York: 28; Gift of the Beate Klarsfeld Foundation, courtesy of Museum of Jewish Heritage, New York: 24; Leo Baeck Institute, New York: cover (top right), 12, 26, 27; Library of Congress: 15; United States Holocaust Memorial Museum: 108; UPI/Corbis-Bettmann: 61, 78, 80, 87, 88, 92, 93, 100, 103 (bottom); Zionist Archives: 107.

Library of Congress Cataloging-in-Publication Data
Fox, Anne L.
    Ten Thousand Children: True stories told by children who escaped the holocaust on the Kindertransport / by Anne L. Fox and Eva Abraham-Podietz.
        p.   cm.
    Summary: Tells the true stories of children who escaped Nazi Germany on the Kindertransport, a rescue mission led by concerned British to save Jewish children from the Holocaust.
    ISBN 0-87441-648-5
    1. Jewish children—Germany—Biography—Juvenile literature. 2. Jews—Germany—History—1933-1945—Juvenile literature. 3. Refugees, Jewish—Great Britain —Biography—Juvenile literature. 4. Jewish children—Great Britain—Biography—Juvenile literature. [1. Jews—Germany—Biography. 2. Refugees—Great Britain.
3. World War, 1939-1945—Personal narratives.] I. Abraham-Podietz, Eva. II. Title.
DS135.G5A1293   1998
940.53'18'083—dc21
[B]   98-33600
                                                                                  CIP
                                                                                   AC

Project Editor: Alison Minion
Book and Cover Design: Howard Levy Design

Copyright ©1999 by Behrman House

Published by Behrman House, Inc.
235 Watchung Avenue
West Orange, NJ 07052

Manufactured in the United States of America

TEN THOUSAND CHILDREN

True stories told by children who escaped
the Holocaust on the Kindertransport

by Anne L. Fox and
Eva Abraham-Podietz

Behrman House, Inc.

Contents

To the Reader

The stories in this book are true. They are about people who were children in Germany during the time of **Adolf Hitler**'s rise to power. Their parents and many of their grandparents had made their home in a country which they loved, and to which they were loyal. Very few of these people talked about what happened to them as children until many years later, when they had children and grandchildren of their own.

Even when they were very young, they were aware of the **anti-Semitism** being spread by Hitler's **Nazi Party**. Eventually all Jews suffered very cruel treatment under his rule. Many were sent to

Hitler, Adolf
head of the German government from 1933 to 1945 and leader of the Nazi Party

anti-Semitism
hostility toward Jews and everything Jewish

Nazi Party
National Socialist German Workers' Party, an anti-Semitic political group led by Adolf Hitler

concentration camp
general name for place where Jews and others were imprisoned and often killed by the Nazis during the Holocaust

ghetto
neighborhood set up by Nazis in which Jews were forced to live in inhumane, over-crowded conditions

Kindertransport
German for *Children's Transport*, the program through which 10,000 children were brought to England

Holocaust
the period of Hitler's rule during which over six million European Jews were killed in the Nazis' organized effort to wipe out all of European Jewry; other groups were also singled out for destruction by the Nazis

concentration camps or **ghettos** where they died from starvation or disease; still others were killed by the brutal Nazis.

Here you will read about children who were lucky. A group of British citizens asked their government for permission to let the children come to England. The children had to make this journey alone, without their parents. This transport of children to England became known as the **Kindertransport**.

The authors of this book were among the nearly 10,000 children who escaped the Nazis as part of the Kindertransport. One of us was eleven and the other twelve years old at the time.

It was very difficult for mothers and fathers to say good-bye to their children. But however painful the parting, parents felt it best for them to leave. They were hoping to be together again very soon; no one could know that there would be a war that would last six long years, and that a reunion with their loved ones would not be possible until it ended. Nor could they know that Hitler planned to destroy all the Jews in Europe, and that eventually six million Jews—over one and a half million of them children—would die in the period of history that has come to be known as the **Holocaust**.

The children who came to England with the Kindertransport had many problems in their new country. Although most British people were kind to them, they missed their families terribly. Everyone hoped that Hitler would lose the war and the children would soon be home again with their parents and relatives.

By the time victory was celebrated, many of the children felt at home in England with their **foster parents**. They still longed to be reunited with their own families, but that was not always possible.

The Kindertransport children were fortunate to be in England during the war years. They worked and studied hard in order to become good citizens of the country that had welcomed them. While many of them stayed in England after the war ended, others left to join family and friends who had been able to escape or survive Nazi rule. Sadly, some of the Kindertransport children found that their parents, siblings, and other relatives had perished in the Holocaust.

The authors of this book want you to try to put yourself in the place of the children whose stories you will read. These true stories were told to us by the **Kinder**, as they still call themselves today. None of them will ever forget what happened to them.

We should always remember the terrible years of the Holocaust. You, too, need to work toward making this a better world, without hatred and war.

Anne and Eva

foster parents
adults who volunteer to take in children whose parents cannot care for them

Kinder
German for *children*

Life under Hitler

Between the years of 1914 and 1918, Germany fought in World War I against France, England, Russia, and the United States. Germany lost the war and was forced to give up some territories and pay enormous sums of money to the countries that had won. As a result, there was great poverty and a shortage of food in Germany. Many people were out of work and, even if they had money, there was little to buy in the stores. Banks and businesses failed.

Amid this suffering, and while the German people struggled with the shame of having lost the war, Adolf Hitler began to organize the Nazi Party. He promised that he would make it possible for everyone to be employed and have enough food. He had no trouble falsely blaming Germany's hard times on the Jews. Jews had lived in Germany for many

Adolf Hitler, addressing a crowd of supporters, gives the Nazi salute.

centuries, and there were Jewish doctors, lawyers, bankers, scientists, teachers, and shopkeepers. Other Jews contributed to the arts as writers, poets, composers, musicians, artists, and actors. Despite all their accomplishments, however, many German

A rally of Hitler's Nazi Party.

people had not fully accepted them as fellow citizens.

In 1933, Hitler and his Nazi Party came to power in Germany. He urged the German people not to be friends with Jews, not to shop at Jewish stores or use the services of Jewish people.

German boys were obligated to join the **Hitler Youth** groups, and girls became members of the **League of German Girls**. They wore brown uniforms with red kerchiefs and swastikas on their armbands. They all had to swear to support the new leader of Germany. Children were told to put loyalty to Hitler above obedience to their own parents. The Nazi Youth group leaders taught them that Germans were a superior "**Aryan**" race, and that Jews were inferior people who only wanted to take their money and destroy their country. Books and posters printed pictures of Jews looking like ugly dwarfs with

Hitler Youth
  group founded by the Nazi Party; it taught German children Nazi ideas, especially hatred of the Jewish people

League of German Girls
  the girls' branch of Hitler Youth

swastika
  an ancient symbol that became the emblem for Hitler's Nazi Party

Aryan
  ethnic type considered pure Germans by the Nazis

black hair and big noses, their hands filled with money.

All Jewish government workers were forced to leave their jobs, and Jewish artists could no longer perform on the stage or play with an orchestra. Books by Jewish authors were burned in big bonfires in the streets. Large signs saying "Jews not wanted" or "Jews forbidden" appeared above the entrances to skating rinks, tennis courts, swimming pools, movie houses, restaurants, and other public places. In the parks, Jewish people were allowed to sit only on benches painted yellow and marked "For Jews only." Parents worried whenever their children went out; one never knew when Nazis or gangs of Hitler Youth would attack anyone they thought was a Jew.

In 1935, Hitler's government passed the **Nuremberg Laws**, which made life even more difficult for Jews. They were deprived of their rights as German citizens. They were not allowed to marry "Aryans." Jewish lawyers and doctors could no longer serve non-Jews. All Jewish children

had to leave German schools and enroll in Jewish schools, which were hastily set up. Nazi gangs smeared Jewish shops with large swastikas and graffiti. They stood guard outside stores and prevented customers from

This anti-Semitic poster from Hitler's Germany reads, "When you see this symbol, know your enemy."

entering. All properties owned by Jews had to be listed with the Nazi authorities, who would then take them over.

Many Jewish people tried to leave

Nuremberg Laws
anti-Jewish laws passed by Hitler in 1935 that deprived Jews of citizenship and forbade them to marry anyone of German blood

Germany, hoping to join relatives in other countries. But in order to **emigrate** they needed a **passport**, as well as permission from the country they wished to enter. The United States had a **quota** that allowed only a limited number of immigrants. Jews wishing to leave Germany had to wait their turn, and for many, their turn never came. Even if they had all the necessary papers, they were not always allowed to take all their belongings. Furthermore, their luggage was carefully inspected before it could be transported, and Jews had to pay large fees to the Nazis in order to ship any valuables found inside their bags. Still, some were lucky enough to get out of Germany in time to be saved from the Holocaust.

emigrate
to leave one's country

passport
official proof of nationality; document needed to travel outside of one's native country

quota
a fixed and limited number of people admitted to a country each year

Caught in a Crowd

COLOGNE
GERMANY

"**W**hat is happening? Why are all these people in the street?" I asked my older sister, Ruth. We were on our way home from school, which was usually only a short walk along a tree-lined, cobblestone street. But today the way was blocked by noisy crowds milling around. I groped for Ruth's hand so I could hold onto her. I was afraid the mob might separate us.

Fuehrer
German for *leader*, the title given to Adolf Hitler

"Hitler is coming! The **Fuehrer** is coming to Cologne," the people were saying. Sure enough, an open car, escorted by other vehicles, could be seen in the distance. A figure was standing up in the open car with his arm raised. It was Adolf Hitler.

Sylvia (left) with her mother and her sister, Ruth.

Hitler and his aides give the Nazi salute.

I was terrified. Ruth tried to keep me calm by squeezing my hand tightly. We felt trapped in the large crowd that had gathered. The excited mass of people pressed toward the edge of the pavement. Holding back the mob were tall men wearing brown Hitler uniforms and high black boots. Swastikas were clearly visible on their sleeves.

"**Sieg Heil!**" they shouted. "Sieg Heil! Sieg Heil!" raising their right arms high to salute their leader. I tried to catch Ruth's eye, but she was desperately trying to make a path for us to escape the crowd. Were we expected to raise our right arm for the hated Hitler salute? I was surprised when in a second Ruth's arm shot up. I must do the same, I thought. After

Sieg Heil
German for *Hail victory*, a Nazi greeting and salute

all, Ruth is older and knows what to do. I also extended my arm into the air. I was afraid to give the Hitler salute, but even more afraid not to. It made me feel disloyal to all the Jews that Hitler hated so much.

When we finally reached home after the motorcade had passed and the crowd had thinned, I was too ashamed to talk about what had happened.

"Mother would not have given the Hitler salute," I confided to Ruth later in the safety of our home. "She has so much courage. Whenever someone says '**Heil Hitler**' to her, she always answers, 'Good day!'"

We had been warned to keep quiet outside the home and not to draw attention to ourselves. I had followed this rule ever since I was six years old. The grown-ups also talked in hushed voices whenever they were in the street. They did not want to be noticed by the roving gangs of Hitler Youth. At home it was safe, but outside it was dangerous. If you were recognized as a Jew, you might be beaten up.

Heil Hitler
German for *Hail Hitler*, greeting among Hitler's followers for "hello" and "good-bye," accompanied by a raised right arm

Sylvia and her older sister, Ruth, were born in Cologne, a very old German town. Their father was a teacher. The two sisters were very close, almost like twins. Sylvia admired her older sister because she was very smart in school. Teachers expected Sylvia to be just as smart as her sister, but Sylvia had to work very hard to get good marks.

In September 1938, the girls and their mother were among many Jews rounded up by the Nazis and sent to a small town in Poland. After a few months living under difficult conditions, the girls were sent to England with the Kindertransport.

The sisters could not stay together with one family, but they visited whenever they could. After leaving her British school at fourteen, Sylvia learned shorthand and typing.

After the war, an aunt who had moved to America found Sylvia's address in England and brought her to New York to live with her. Sylvia dared not ask what happened to her parents; she was afraid to hear bad news. Her aunt did not tell her for quite a while that her parents had died in a concentration camp.

Sylvia worked as a secretary in New York, married an American, and raised a daughter, Melanie.

The Orange

Would you believe me if I told you that an orange was the best birthday present I ever got? And that I got it in an awful place called Zbaszyn, where we had only straw to sleep on and nothing to eat? That orange was a miracle.

But first let me tell you what brought us—my mother, my younger sister Sylvia, and me—to a small Polish town on the German-Polish border in the middle of October.

My father was born in Antwerp, Belgium; my mother in Cracow, Poland. They met and married in Germany, where they made a home, and where my sister and I were born. We thought of ourselves as good Germans, but the Nazis never gave us German passports. They considered us Polish.

ZBASZYN
POLAND

One day a man from the **Gestapo** came to our door, asking for Father. Whenever someone in a Nazi uniform came to the door, we were fearful.

"He is not home," my mother told him, her voice trembling. "He went to visit his mother in Belgium."

Two days later Mother received an order to come to the police station with us. We were allowed to bring only a small bag with a few belongings. It was the last time we saw our home.

We were pushed onto a train with hundreds of other people. After an overnight journey, we had to get out at a small border town between Germany and Poland. We were very hungry and tired. Mother put us to sleep on the waiting room table of the railway station. Winter comes early in Eastern Europe, and I remember it was freezing cold that day. More and more trains arrived, unloading more and more people. They could not even find enough space to lie down.

The next morning we were taken to **barracks**. We were each given a bowl of thin soup, a piece of stale bread, and straw to sleep on. We had to get water for drinking and washing from a pump. During that time many got sick, and some died.

zum Kaffee bei sich zu sehen.

A birthday party invitation from Ruth's childhood in Cologne.

Gestapo
German Secret Police, who often terrorized people on behalf of the Nazis

barracks
building or group of buildings used to house soldiers

I had my eleventh birthday in November, while we were in Zbaszyn. If we had been at home, Mother would have baked me a huge birthday cake and decorated it with flowers and candles—one for every year, plus one to grow on. My friends would have come all dressed up in their party clothes, the girls with ribbons in their hair.

"Happy birthday, Ruth," they'd say, and extend their hands, and each one would give me a beautifully wrapped present, tied with bows. We would play games and eat cake.

But there would be no birthday celebration in Zbaszyn.

Instead, Mother handed me an orange. I didn't know where she got it. I couldn't believe that she had found the precious fruit in this place! I could not bear to eat it, or to share it with anyone. So I kept it. Each day I would say to myself, "I'll eat it today." But I didn't. Oranges don't last forever, and finally mine turned rotten and I had to throw it away. But I would always remember this very special present!

Eventually, we were able to leave Zbaszyn with the help of my aunt in Cracow. I never saw another orange until I came to England with the Kindertransport.

Like her sister, Sylvia, Ruth was born in Cologne. Ruth was a year older than Sylvia and very protective of her. People did not think that they were sisters because Sylvia had fair skin like their mother, while Ruth had dark hair and eyes like their father. Because of her darker coloring, Nazi youths often called her "dirty Jew" and chased her.

One day, before the sisters left Germany, a gang of Hitler Youth followed them and called them names. Ruth tried to protect Sylvia and pulled her away from the crowd, but Ruth fell and hit her head on the curb. Sylvia tried to find help. Ruth had to be taken to a Jewish doctor, since Jewish people were not allowed to go to a German hospital.

Ruth studied to become a nurse in England.

In October 1938, without warning, all Jews of Polish origin were brought to German police stations and loaded onto trains to Poland. Ruth, her mother, and her sister were among them. A few months later, Ruth and Sylvia were able to leave Poland with the Kindertransport.

Ruth studied nursing at a hospital in England. She seldom saw her sister, Sylvia, because they were separated by many miles. Ruth died when she was only eighteen from a tumor in her head. Her doctors thought that it was caused by the injury she received when she hit her head while running away from the Nazis. Losing Ruth was very sad for Sylvia, who was left all alone.

A Lasting Friendship

My name is Anne and I want to tell you about my best friend, Dorit. She lived in Germany during the war. She always called me "Mickey" because I would put my hands on my head and squeak like Mickey Mouse in the movies. Dorit and I went to the same elementary school in Berlin.

Dorit was an only child and lived with her parents in a small apartment only two blocks from me. My family's apartment was

BERLIN GERMANY

Dorit (center), with her father and her best friend, Anne.

much bigger than Dorit's. It had a long hallway where we often played, danced, and tumbled. Our favorite game was getting dressed up. We would choose what to wear from a big box filled with treasures that was kept at the top of the linen closet. It contained Mother's old dresses, slips, costume jewelry, hats, and scarves. There was even a thick braid of hair Mother had saved when she decided to have her hair cut short. It was great fun to play make-believe.

Dorit and I shared our holidays with each other. Dorit's family was Christian, so they celebrated Christmas and Easter. I helped trim her family's Christmas tree and painted eggs with them at Easter. She lit the menorah with us at Ḥannukah, and came over to eat matzah and other goodies at Passover.

When Hitler came to power, he made many rules for Jews. We were no longer allowed the same rights and freedoms as other people. Jewish children had to leave their old schools and go to Jewish schools. I had to go to a new school in a different part of the city. Every day but Saturday, I had to ride the elevated train to get there.

I missed my friend Dorit. We had such good times together, and being apart was hard. I would never have a best friend like her again. On the rare times that she came to see me, she did not use the front entrance, but instead came up the iron staircase leading to the back door. This was used only by delivery men and trash collectors. Since Germans had been told by Hitler not to talk to Jews, Dorit didn't want anyone to see her visiting me.

"Whenever you see me wearing the Hitler Youth uniform," she explained, "pretend that you don't know me. I am not allowed to talk to you." I knew that Dorit did not believe what she was taught in the Hitler Youth meetings she had to attend. But still my feelings were hurt, even though I tried to understand.

A few months after I had to switch schools, I left Germany with the Kindertransport. Dorit continued to visit my mother by sneaking up the iron staircase. She brought chocolates, which my mother sent to me in England.

Although Dorit and I did not meet again until after the war, we often thought about each other.

A Hitler Youth ID card issued in Munich on December 22, 1937.

Dorit

Dorit's parents did not agree with Hitler's ideas and never belonged to the Nazi Party, but Dorit joined the girls at school who wore the Hitler Youth uniform. She wanted to be like the other girls.

During the war, Berlin was bombed heavily by the British and American forces, and schools were closed in order to protect the schoolchildren. Dorit and her mother went to live in the country, where Dorit went to a new school. She later studied to become a teacher. After the war her family returned to a bombed-out Berlin. The front of their apartment house had been badly damaged, but the back of the building was still standing.

Dorit with her kittens, Biggy and Tiny, in 1984.

Dorit taught English, history, and psychology. While visiting England to improve her English, she was told that her friend Anne had married and moved to America. She found Anne's address and wrote to her. Anne was happy to hear from her friend and answered her letter.

Dorit retired after 41 years of teaching. She lives in a cheerful apartment in Berlin, which she shares with her three Siamese cats: Tiny, Biggy, and Jenny. She often writes to Anne, and they have visited each other. They still exchange gifts at holiday times.

CHAPTER 2

Kristallnacht

As Hitler's rule continued, life became increasingly difficult for the Jews in Germany. Hitler's laws forced many Jewish people to leave their jobs, and Jews found it harder and harder to make a living. The Nazis took over Jewish businesses without paying the owners. Every day Jews were beaten in the street, and many men were taken to concentration camps. Mothers and children were left alone. They worried about the men, but could do little to help.

Only those who could show a **visa** that admitted them to another country were allowed to leave Germany. Although many hoped that Hitler's rule would not last, a large number of Jews continued to try to leave. They were willing to go to any country that would accept them.

The world did not heed the signs that Hitler was preparing for war. Germans had to recycle toothpaste tubes, aluminum foil, and other metal objects. The iron railings around patches of grass disappeared. The

visa
a document granting permission to enter a country

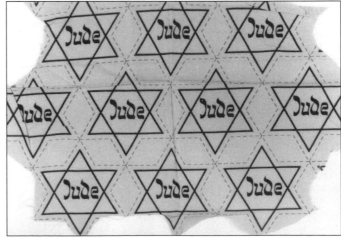

Jews were forced to sew a Star of David on their clothing to identify themselves as Jews.

Hundreds of synagogues were set on fire during Kristallnacht.

children missed balancing on them for fun; they did not know that the railings were being melted down to make guns. Signs soon appeared pointing out **air raid shelters**. Whenever howling sirens signaled an **air raid drill**, everyone was forced to clear the streets and take shelter.

In October 1936, Italy signed a friendship pact with Hitler. One year later, Japan also became an ally of Germany. Neither Britain nor France nor America protested when, in 1936, the Nazis occupied the Rhineland, a territory that belonged to France. Two years later, in the spring of 1938, Hitler's army occupied Austria and took over the Sudetenland, part of Czechoslovakia.

Other countries did not respond to the Nazis' cruel treatment of the Jews who now lived under their rule in the

air raid shelter
a place to protect people from bombs

air raid drill
exercise to practice emergency procedure in case of a bombing attack

Jewish refugees board the *St. Louis*. After being sent back to Europe, many of its passengers perished in the Holocaust.

Kristallnacht
German for *night of broken glass.* November 9–10, 1938, when the Nazis burned synagogues, destroyed Jewish-owned businesses, and sent many Jews to concentration camps

vandalism
willful destruction of property

captured territories. Although many Americans knew about the hardships these Jews were suffering, the American government did nothing. Nor did it increase the quota of Germans to be admitted into the United States.

The night of November 9–10, 1938, will never be forgotten by the Jews who lived through it in Germany. It became known as **Kristallnacht** (night of broken glass). On this night, the Nazis set fire to almost all the synagogues in Germany and destroyed and looted many Jewish-owned stores. Jewish homes were broken into, and people were terrorized and beaten. After the **vandalism**, 30,000 men—husbands, fathers, brothers, and sons—were taken to police stations and then to concentration camps.

The world remained silent as they took notice of these events and watched Hitler's military strength grow. Very few countries opened their doors to Jewish people. In May 1939, when a ship called the *St. Louis* tried to land in Cuba with Jewish **refugees** aboard, it was not allowed to dock. The ship and its passengers were sent back to Europe.

Hitler's laws continued to make life unbearable for the Jews. They were forced to sew a yellow Jewish star onto their clothing with the word *Jude*— the German word for "Jew"—printed in black. The purpose was to embarrass the Jews. It was illegal for them to appear in public without wearing the star. The Nazis closed Jewish bank accounts, and Jews were made to turn in all their jewelry and valuables at the police station. They were not even allowed to keep their pets.

The German people saw what was happening in their country, but very few spoke up. Some feared punishment. Others liked Hitler's plans for a stronger and richer Germany. And still others supported Nazi anti-Semitism.

refugee
one who flees to another country

A Scary Night

My name is Karla, and I lived in Berlin, the capital of Germany. I will never forget what happened when I was eleven years old. I attended the Jewish middle school, since Hitler had ruled that no Jewish children could go to German schools anymore. My new school was a long way from my home. Every morning, I walked to the elevated train station and rode about thirty minutes to the other end of town. The time passed quickly because there were other Jewish girls who boarded at stations along the way.

BERLIN
GERMANY

On one November night, our lives and the lives of all Jews in Germany changed forever. That night, the Nazis smashed all the storefronts of Jewish businesses, beat the owners, broke into homes, destroyed property, and took many Jewish men and boys to the police station. They were arrested even though they had done nothing wrong. The Nazis made up charges against them and sent them to work camps. Most synagogues in Germany were set on fire, and the police and firefighters were ordered not to help the victims or put out the fires. The date was November 9, 1938, and the night became known as Kristallnacht, "night of broken glass."

Karla, still in Berlin, models her party dress.

I remember being awakened that night by loud banging and the sound of glass shattering. My family, including my younger brothers, Dan and Ernest, huddled together in fear. Father bolted the front door while Mother tried to comfort us. We shivered with terror.

Suddenly there was a knock on the door. Everybody jumped up in panic. Had the dreaded Gestapo come for us?

"Who is there?" asked Father, his voice trembling.

"Please open the door," begged a woman in a shaky voice. Father unlocked the door. There stood the two little elderly ladies, Miss Elsa and Miss Anna, who owned the stationery store across the street. They told us that their store window had been smashed by a gang in Nazi uniforms, and that most of the merchandise had been destroyed or stolen. They fled their apartment behind the store in their nightclothes. Both were shivering with fright and cold.

I knew the two ladies well because I had always bought all my school supplies at their store. They were kind and generous, and had often placed a free eraser or an extra pencil in my bag of purchases. Mother tried to calm the ladies and brewed strong coffee for all the adults. Then she put my sleepy brothers back to bed. I pulled the covers tightly over my head, but I could not fall back to sleep.

My parents did not let me go to school the next morning, but a few days later I was allowed to leave the house. I had to walk very carefully to avoid stepping on the broken glass that still littered the sidewalk. The elevated train I took to school passed close by the synagogue I had attended with my family on Shabbat and on holidays. Whenever I passed the building on the train, I always looked for the dome. What a shock it was to see that

Hoping to get out of Germany before it was too late, Jews lined up outside a Berlin travel agency immediately after Kristallnacht.

the beautiful building had almost completely burned down! The ashes were still smoldering, and as the train sped by, I caught a glimpse of a few charred walls left standing. I felt angry and saddened. I couldn't understand why the Nazis would do such a thing. What had the Jews done to them?

Soon after this terrible night, my father tried to get a visa to go to America or any other country that would admit us. My brothers and I were sent to England with the Kindertransport. My parents eventually emigrated to Argentina.

Many Jewish homes, businesses, and synagogues were destroyed.

ARGENTINA

Karla left Germany with her brothers on the Kinder-transport. She stayed with an English family who sent her to school and treated her as if she were their own child. Still, Karla longed to live with her own family again. Her wish came true after the war, when she and her brothers were able to join their parents in Argentina. Once reunited with her family, Karla had to learn yet another language—this time, Spanish—and to get used to a new way of life once again. She married a dental technician who had also fled Germany. Her parents found it very difficult to get used to life in Argentina, and had trouble learning Spanish. When Karla and her husband had a baby, Karla's parents helped take care of their grandson. Karla died a few years ago.

Karla was reunited with her family after the war.

The Hardware Store

My father owned a hardware store in a small town near Frankfurt, Germany. Both my parents worked there, as did my older sister, Edith. I loved to help out in the store. There were so many interesting things on the shelves—tools, paint, glue, nails, pots and pans, and buckets. I learned where everything was kept, so I could help out someday.

Finally, I had my chance. Father was on a trip to buy supplies for the store, Edith was in school, and Mother asked me

to mind the store while she ran an errand. I was delighted when the bell over the door rang and a customer entered.

"Can I help you?" I asked, just as I had heard my parents say. The lady wanted to buy a mixing bowl. I knew where all the bowls were kept, and I arranged a dozen bowls of different sizes, colors, and shapes on the counter. I felt very grown-up. The customer finally selected one. Mother returned in time to take the money. She was very proud of me.

One day on my way home from school, two boys in Hitler Youth uniforms came up behind me. At first I was not scared, but when they blocked my way, I tried to run away.

"Hey, aren't you a Jew girl?" they asked me with a mocking smile.

The ruins of a Berlin synagogue after Kristallnacht.

"You don't look like a Jew." At the Hitler Youth meetings they were told that all Jews had dark hair and eyes and hooked noses. I had blond hair and blue eyes. They knew that the owner of the hardware store was Jewish, but they were not sure that I was his daughter.

"Doesn't your father own the hardware store?" they questioned me. I nodded my head to say yes. I tried to escape, but not before the two bullies had pushed me down and called me "dirty Jew." My knee was hurt and bleeding. I ran home, crying.

Soon afterwards, the terrible night of Kristallnacht happened. My mother, my sister, and I heard loud voices and

laughter, followed by the sound of breaking glass. Next we heard the crash of things being smashed on the floor downstairs. The noise was awful.

"Quick, up to the attic!" Mother said, pulling us after her. We hid together all night and most of the next day in the attic until it was quiet again. Only then did we dare go downstairs to look at the ruined store. What a mess it was!

We all cried. Mother consoled us. She was thankful that we were not harmed. We did not know why Father still had not come home from his buying trip. Mother found out that the Gestapo had taken him to a **work camp**. When he came home a short time later, I hardly recognized him. He was so thin and his hair had been shaved off.

Mother knew she had to save her children by sending us out of Germany. Soon after that terrible night she found out about the Kindertransport. Edith began to pack a suitcase. Mother wanted her to go first because she was the oldest, but at seventeen, she was too old to be accepted. I was only nine. Mother arranged for me to take her place.

Before I knew what was happening, Mother gave me Edith's suitcase, kissed me good-bye, and put me on the train to Holland. I was almost as big as my sister. If Edith's clothes were too big for me, she explained, I would grow into them.

Mother and Edith were not able to leave Germany. They were sent to a concentration camp.

work camp
a type of concentration camp where Nazis forced their prisoners to do slave labor

When Susie arrived in England, she was sent to live in several foster homes. She tried to follow her mother's advice to be good, helpful, and grateful, but it was hard. One family who took care of her in Coventry, north of London, was very strict and beat her for being disobedient. She kept all her unhappiness to herself.

Coventry was very badly bombed by the Germans during the war, so Susie moved to a **hostel** in Birmingham, where she was sent to work although she was only fourteen years old.

After the war ended, Susie was told that her mother and sister had survived the war. Her father, however, had died. Her mother and Edith had to regain their health and wait for their emigration papers to America. Meanwhile, an aunt and uncle who had gone to America before the war asked Susie to come and live with them. Susie did not want to leave England, but she thought it best to join them.

hostel
temporary residence for those who need a place to stay

As soon as she arrived in the United States, Susie arranged for her mother and sister to come to New York. At last they were together again. Susie and Edith became very close friends. Their mother, however, had to get to know Susie again; she remembered her as a small child, but now she was a teenager. Living together was not always easy.

Susie married Walter in 1950, and they bought an egg farm in New Jersey. They have three children and four grandchildren. Susie's sister, Edith, settled in California. Her mother lived to be 84 years old.

Susie and her husband, Walter, in 1996.

The Big Fire

As long as I live, I will never forget Kristallnacht. That terrible night will always stick in my mind, although I was only a small child at the time.

My mother and I were visiting my aunt and uncle. They lived across the street from the Broder Synagogue, where my grandfather was the cantor. We were sitting around the table drinking tea when we heard loud banging outside. It sounded like heavy objects crashing to the ground, and soon there was the sound of breaking glass. People were screaming and there was shrill laughter.

We didn't know what was going on. I was very frightened, especially when my aunt turned the lights off. In the darkness we huddled together seeking comfort from each other. I held on tightly to my mother. I was trembling with fear. Mother was shaking, too. I could feel it as I hid in her arms. My uncle

Vera's first day of school, 1932. She is holding a zuckertüte, a candy-filled cone given to German children on their first day of school.

Eight-year-old Vera at a family picnic, 1933.

cautiously crept to the window and peered out through the curtains. Suddenly the room was lit up by blinding light, and shadows danced on the ceiling.

"They have made a big fire," my uncle said. He motioned for us to come to the window to see a blazing bonfire in front of the synagogue. Mother recognized the black-covered books that were being tossed into the flames.

"They are burning our prayer books," she whispered in horror. "No, not the Torah, too!" She stood rooted to the window, watching the SS men tossing the Holy Scrolls into the fire. The scrolls did not catch fire immediately. I learned later that parchment, on which the Torah is written, does not burn easily.

There was much shouting and laughing among the SS men,

SS
Nazi security
squad also known
as "Blackshirts"; a
powerful military
arm of the Nazis
that protected
Hitler and the
Party and that
oversaw the con-
centration camps

as though this were just a big joke. All we could do was watch, trembling with fear and helplessness.

When the doorbell rang, we all jumped. My aunt slowly opened the door. It was my other aunt and uncle, who lived a short distance away. They were terribly upset. The **SS** had broken into their home, hacked the furniture to pieces, and smashed the dishes and crystal. Then they set the house on fire. My uncle and aunt had escaped through the cellar door. Both were crying. It was the first time I had ever seen a grown man cry.

Our family listened to our shortwave radio all night. We hoped to hear that America or other countries had heard about Kristallnacht and would open their doors to the Jewish people who were trapped in Germany. But this good news did not arrive.

A few weeks later, my five cousins and I left for England on the Kindertransport. Our lives were saved.

UPDATE:
Vera

After Kristallnacht, Vera's uncle arranged for her and five of her cousins to leave on the Kindertransport. One of Vera's aunts sent her three children—ages five, three, and six months old—to England. A fourteen-year-old cousin was told to take care of them on the journey. Vera was twelve when she left home.

In England, all the children were taken care of by Christian foster parents. Vera stayed with a kind family for eight years, but when she turned 21, she decided to move closer to her remaining Jewish relatives, who had emigrated to America. She had received very little education in England, and decided to attend classes at night in New York.

One summer, Vera worked at an overnight camp, where she met a fellow counselor whom she later married. They have two daughters and three grandchildren. Vera is active in her synagogue in New Jersey and does volunteer work in the community. She speaks often to children of all races and religions and tells them, "Accept differences and respect your fellow human beings. Do not hate anyone for being different."

Vera and her husband, Seymour, in 1994.

Preparing to Leave

A British newspaper advertisment in support of the Kindertransport.

Quakers
a religious group, also known as the Society of Friends

Jews in England were alarmed to hear of the burning of the synagogues on Kristallnacht and the destruction of Jewish property by the Nazis. Several Jewish organizations, together with church groups and the **Quakers**, begged the British government to admit Jewish children from Germany and the other countries Hitler had invaded. They felt that the Jewish children had to be rescued, and they wanted to bring as many of them as possible to England right away.

England's government granted permission to admit children without a passport, with certain conditions. The children had to come alone, without their parents, and could be no older than seventeen. The nation's leaders feared that older children would take jobs away from the British people. The Jewish organizations involved promised to raise the necessary money and to seek shelter for the children.

Organizers of this rescue effort went to Germany to ask permission of the Nazis to let Jewish children leave with the transports, which became known as the Kindertransports. The Nazis agreed, provided the children took no valuables out of the country.

As soon as word of the Kindertransports spread, many parents were anxious to register their children. Offices were hurriedly set up in Berlin, Germany; Vienna, Austria; Prague, Czechoslovakia, and other big cities. Though it was difficult for parents to send their children away, they feared for their children's safety under Nazi rule.

Those who were accepted for the Kindertransport had very little time to prepare for the trip. They were allowed to pack only as much as they could carry, forcing them to make difficult decisions. They had to choose what to pack and what to leave behind. It was important to take warm clothing and enough underwear, socks, and sleepwear. Favorite toys and books were left

sons and daughters advice on how to behave in a strange country among strange people. They worried how their children would be treated by their English foster families. It took a lot of courage for parents to part with their children, but they did not want

Passport issued to a Jewish child in Hamburg, December 1938.

behind on shelves. For parents, these things became constant reminders of their children so far away. Many children slipped some photographs of their families into their suitcases, to remind them of their loved ones. These photos became treasured possessions.

Mothers and fathers gave their

to let them see how much it hurt to part with them. Besides, many of them hoped to be reunited soon, either in England, in America, or in any other country that would admit them.

When the first Kindertransport left Germany on December 6, 1938, few people expected that war would break out.

Little "Grown-Up"

Papi
affectionate
German word
for *Father*

"Oh, dear," said my mother, hanging up the telephone. "Aunt Gerti just told me that we must go as soon as possible to register you for the Kindertransport. But I cannot get away today. I have so much to do. Besides, **Papi** wrote that he would call me this morning. Maybe he has good news and finally got the visas for both of us."

Eva poses with
her teddy bear.

HAMBURG
GERMANY

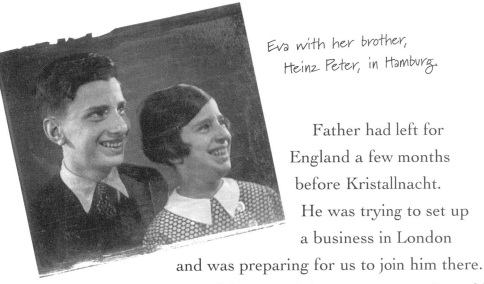

Eva with her brother,
Heinz Peter, in Hamburg.

Father had left for
England a few months
before Kristallnacht.
He was trying to set up
a business in London
and was preparing for us to join him there.

Mother told me that if the visas did not come soon, I would have to go alone to England with the Kindertransport.

"I can go by myself to the Kindertransport office and register my name, **Mutti**," I suggested. "You could send me in a cab. I will be all right."

Mother was worried about sending me by myself, since the office was in another part of Hamburg. But I was eleven years old and felt quite capable of going alone. Finally, Mother phoned for a taxi. She gave the driver the address, with strict instructions to wait for me outside the office and to bring me straight back home.

I thought this was a great adventure. I had never been in a cab by myself before. Like a queen, I settled in the spacious backseat, feeling very grown-up.

Mutti
affectionate
German word
for *Mother*

Eva (far left), aged three, with her older
brother and cousins on their first day of school.

With her brother and their parents in London, July 1947.

Frau
German for *Mrs.*

A huge crowd had gathered at the entrance of the building. Women and children spilled into the street, anxiously waiting for their turn to get on the Kindertransport list. I pushed through the crowd to get to the head of the line. "Excuse me," I mumbled, "my mother is waiting for me. She must be up front. I am supposed to meet her." The women stared at me as I made my way to the head of the line.

I had almost reached the table in front where several men and women sat with pens in hand. There were lots of papers in front of them. All eyes turned to glare at me. "My mother must be in this line," I explained to the people behind the table. "I was going to meet her here. My name is Eva Rosenbaum."

"**Frau** Rosenbaum!" one of the men called loudly. "Frau Rosenbaum!" But of course there was no response.

"Where is your mother?" he wanted to know.

Without answering him, I pulled my passport out of my pocket, and without a word, the man put my name on the list, right then and there.

Pleased with myself, I squeezed my way back through the crowd. The taxi driver was waiting for me. Once again, I made myself comfortable in the backseat of the cab. "Drive through the park," I ordered the driver, "and please go past the synagogue."

I had seen the flames and smoke rising on Kristallnacht but had not seen the building since. I felt so sad to find the familiar synagogue in ruins. My parents had taken me there every Shabbat and on holidays. I had sung in the children's choir.

The driver took me home. Mutti was relieved that I had returned safe and sound. I was very proud that I had been able to register for the Kindertransport by myself.

I left for England ten days later.

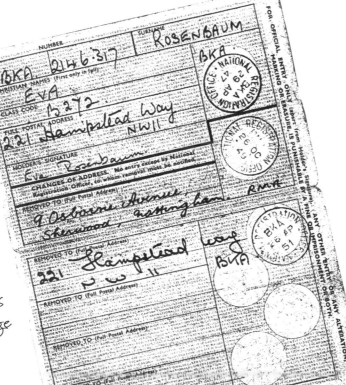

Eva's English identity card. A new card was issued with each change of address.

ISRAEL

Eva's father was already in England when she arrived with the Kindertransport in December 1938. She could not stay with him because he lived in just one room and had to work every day, so Eva was sent to live with a British foster family. Although she was only eleven years old, her foster mother told her to take care of the couple's two-year-old daughter, Adrienne.

Shortly before war broke out, Eva's mother finally received her visa to come to England. The family rented a large apartment in London, and Eva was able to join her parents. But this reunion lasted only a short time, because Eva and her classmates were sent to the safety of the countryside. The British expected the Germans to bomb London. Eva was sent to Northampton, a city north of London, where she lived in four different foster homes. In 1942, Eva moved back to London to be reunited with her parents.

Eva settled in Philadelphia with her husband, David.

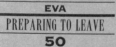

After the war, she went to college and became a teacher and social worker. Eva counseled concentration camp survivors in England, Israel, and Brazil, and finally came to live in the United States in 1959.

Most of the stories in this book were told to Eva by people who had come to England on the Kindertransport when they were children. She recorded them on tapes, which are now stored in Gratz College in Philadelphia. Anyone studying the Holocaust can listen to them.

Eva is retired and lives in Philadelphia with her husband, David. They have five children and five grandchildren.

Marta

On Her Own

There it stood: the brown suitcase. A constant reminder that the day of good-byes was getting closer. The suitcase was so ugly.

"I wish it was real leather," I thought, "and not cheap imitation." But Mother had assured me that this suitcase was much lighter and easier for me to carry than a leather one.

A typical German classroom, 1933

"Can I take my doll?" I asked Mother.

"No, Marta," she replied. "It is too bulky. I'll send it to you in England. Take a stuffed animal instead." I was not happy to leave the doll behind. The doll's big blue eyes reminded me of my favorite aunt Kate.

There was much to do before the journey. Dresses had to be tried on at the dressmaker's, and Mother took me to buy underwear, stockings, and shoes.

"But, Mutti," I complained, "these things are too big on me." I also objected to the long ribbed stockings that Mother packed in the suitcase.

"I always wear kneesocks to school," I insisted. "These stockings are for babies. I am ten years old."

"It is cold and damp in England," Mother replied. "Your clothes may be a bit too big right now, but you are growing and they will fit you for a while." I was puzzled. Hadn't Father told me that he and Mother would soon join me in England?

I did not want to leave my family and my friends, but on the other hand, it would be an adventure to travel by train and ship to England. I had been studying English at school. I knew how to say "How are you," "I don't understand," "please," and "thank you." My English teacher had taught us all about the King and Queen and the two princesses who lived in **Buckingham Palace**.

Buckingham Palace
Palace in London where the King and Queen of England live

Here is the list of do's and don'ts which Mother gave me:

- Be polite — always say "please" and "thank you."
- Eat whatever you are given, even if it is strange and unlike our food at home.
- Do as you are told.
- Don't talk back to adults.
- Always be helpful, and grateful for all you receive.

I thought that Mother really didn't have to tell me all that.

Mother also reminded me to brush my teeth regularly, to wash behind my ears, and to always hang up my clothes. She packed a small sewing kit and showed me how to sew on a button and let down a hem.

We went to a big department store, where Mother bought me a brown tweed coat with a fur collar for the journey. It came almost to my ankles. The curly fur collar was so soft next to my face, and I felt quite grown-up wearing the coat. I did not know at the time that I would wear it for many years, even after it had become shabby and worn.

Mother sent my doll to England in a big package. I wrote to my parents every week until the war broke out and we could no longer send letters or receive mail from Germany. Although they tried very hard, my parents were not able to leave Germany.

Marta tried hard to follow the advice she was given, even though it was difficult. She was very unhappy in the foster homes to which she was sent. At first, she lived with two elderly sisters. She tried to be helpful, but it seemed that they were never satisfied with anything she did. They rarely talked to her. Marta wrote in her diary how lonely and homesick she was. When one of the sisters became ill, Marta was moved to another foster home, a family with four young children. Marta had to baby-sit for them, and hardly had time to do her schoolwork.

After Marta left school at the age of fourteen, she learned typing and shorthand to earn money so she could live on her own. Marta hoped to be reunited with her parents and planned to work to support them. But she never saw them again. They died in a concentration camp.

Marta married an Englishman, and together they began a new life in Canada.

Marta, at age fourteen, in England.

DECEMBER 6, 1938–SEPTEMBER 2, 1939

The Journey

The Hess children carried their instruments on their way to England, December 1938.

chaperone
an older person who accompanies young people to ensure their safety

Children who were to leave with the Kindertransport gathered at railway stations on the day of their departure to England. As many as 200 children might leave together on a single transport, though sometimes the groups were much smaller. Parents were not allowed on the platform; sad good-byes had to be said in waiting rooms. There were many tight hugs and faces wet with tears.

The Nazis ordered many of the Kindertransports to leave on Saturdays. This was especially cruel, because it forced Jews to break their religious laws and travel on Shabbat, which is observed as a day of rest.

Since the parents were not allowed to accompany their children, **chaperones** took care of them on the journey. These chaperones were young Jewish men and women who had volunteered to accompany the children to England, although they were not permitted to stay there, and had to return to Germany. Many of them did not survive the Holocaust.

Most of the children traveled by train through Holland to Hook van Holland, a Dutch **port**. They were fed and comforted by Dutch citizens at stations along the way. Sometimes the children needed a place to sleep until a ferry was available to take them across the **English Channel** to England. A few Kindertransports sailed on large passenger ships from Hamburg, a German port on the **North Sea**. During this two-day journey, the children had to sleep in cabins on the boat. The rough waters of the English Channel are especially choppy in the winter, and most of the children suffered miserably from seasickness.

Once they reached a port in England, the children were taken by train to London. Some were met by relatives or foster parents, while others were sent to hostels or schools. The rest rode a bus to an empty summer camp called Dovercourt, not far from the English Channel they had just crossed.

North Sea
a body of water that connects to the English Channel

port
a sheltered place on the ocean or the mouth of a river with deep enough water to allow ships to come close to shore

English Channel
the waters that divide England from Germany, Holland, Belgium, and France

Emotional parents wave good-bye to their children.

Kurt

The Baby

Even small children were sent alone on the Kindertransport. Everyone had to wear a cardboard identification tag.

I was almost too old to be put on the Kindertransport, because my seventeenth birthday was coming up soon. My father owned a glove factory in Dresden, and I worked there after I graduated from the Jewish high school. I had really wanted to go to college, but Jews were not admitted.

I hoped to get work in England, and to find a way to bring my parents out of Nazi Germany. I had packed my own suitcase and was ready to leave. But why did I have to wear that silly cardboard tag around my neck? I was told that all the children on the Kindertransport had to tie a cardboard tag with their identification number around their neck to make sure that no one got lost during the trip. I had to follow the rules, I suppose.

The day I left for England, I hugged and kissed my parents good-bye at the station. "Good luck," they said. "Take care of yourself. We're glad that you can go to England. We hope to see you soon."

When I boarded the train, I settled myself in a window seat and looked around. Most of the children were much younger than I. There was a lot of loud crying and screaming, which annoyed me. The whistle blew and the conductor lifted his red flag, signaling that the train was about to leave the station. I leaned out the open window to get a last glance at my parents, who were waving good-bye, when suddenly a woman ran up and handed me a large bundle.

"Give her to my sister at the station!" she screamed over the noise of the departing train. "My sister will pick her up in Holland."

I was puzzled. I didn't know what she was talking about. I sat down and started to unwrap the bundle and discovered

that she had handed me a baby! It was a little girl, warmly dressed and tightly wrapped in a pink blanket. A note with a name and address written in large letters was pinned to her clothes.

My first thought was, "What will I do with a baby?" I had no younger brothers or sisters, and I had never even held a baby before. Well, not to worry, I assured myself. So far, so good. The baby was fast asleep. The Dutch border was only a few hours away. I hoped the woman's sister would claim the baby at the station.

I leaned back in my seat with the sleeping baby cradled in my arms. What if she woke up and started to cry? I did not have a bottle or a diaper. I felt responsible for this bundle that I had been given. When one of the girls in the compartment wanted to hold the baby, I refused.

Just before the train crossed the border into Holland, two gruff luggage inspectors in Nazi uniforms came into our compartment and made us open our suitcases. They dug in our belongings looking for valuables. The children's clothes were strewn all over the compartment. I worried that the loud voices of the Nazis would wake the sleeping baby, but she did not stir.

When we finally reached the Dutch border town, everyone was relieved. I immediately spotted a young woman looking into every compartment. I called out the name written on the note. The woman ran up and took the child from me.

"Thank you so much," she said. "May God bless you." Then she was gone. I saw her disappear with her bundle. I felt as though I had lost a friend. I wanted to shout after the woman, to tell her to take good care of the child and to let me know how she was getting along. After all, I had been her caretaker, if only for a few hours. Someone had trusted me with a human life.

A group of Jewish children after their arrival
at the Liverpool Street Station in London, 1939.

UPDATE:

Kurt

When Kurt arrived in England, he was sent to live in a hostel. He soon found a job in a factory in London. Eventually, he located relatives in America, who sent him a ticket to New York. There, he passed the Civil Service examination and was placed in a tax office, where he worked until his retirement.

Kurt married, and has two sons and four grandchildren. He will never forget the baby he took care of, and he often wonders if she survived the Holocaust when Hitler's armies invaded Holland.

Kurt's parents did not survive, but his sister escaped to Switzerland, where she now makes her home.

The Wristwatch

The early morning was still dark when my parents and I started out for the train station. I carried a single knapsack with my belongings. My parents had told me that the children who were going on the Kindertransport were allowed to pack only as much as they could carry. My knapsack was heavy because it was stuffed full with warm clothes for winter. I packed a few games and books, but nothing of value.

It's strange, but I don't remember much of the good-byes. Memory is peculiar, and we often forget the things that were unpleasant or sad. All I remember is that there were lots of children, but I did not know a soul. In a way, I was looking forward to the trip. I had never been on a ferryboat before. I wondered if England looked like Germany, and if I would be able to use the few words of English my mother had taught me.

It was a long trip to the Dutch border. The children did not talk much. Everybody was either sleeping, eating the food they had brought, or simply staring miserably into space. They found it hard to understand that they were going to a strange place where they would be far away from their parents. Some of the younger ones were sobbing quietly. An older girl took a five-year-old boy on her lap to comfort him.

Suddenly the train came to a stop. Outside we heard loud German voices. The door of our compartment was thrown open.

"Luggage inspection!" I heard them shout. Everyone trembled with fear. The older children scrambled to get the suitcases and knapsacks from the luggage racks above their seats. I remembered just in time that I was wearing a watch my uncle had given me on my last birthday. It wasn't gold and probably not worth much, but it was precious to me. I didn't want them to take it, so I slipped it all the way up my arm under the sleeve of my sweater.

The Nazi inspectors had no patience with the children. "Open up!" they ordered. "**Schnell**!" We did as we were

schnell
German for *quick*

told. They looked for gold chains, bracelets, and rings. One little girl had to give up her thin gold necklace with its Star of David. She begged them to let her keep it, but they only laughed. They told us to lift our arms above our heads, and I prayed that my watch would stay in place. I was lucky— the watch didn't slip. To this day, I have always kept that watch, even after it broke and couldn't be fixed.

When the train finally crossed the Dutch border, we were all very happy, and some of us cheered loudly. At the station, a group of Dutch ladies welcomed us and gave us hot chocolate. We were grateful for the snack and relieved to be out of Germany and far away from the hateful Nazis.

Peter lived in a boys' hostel in London and went to the local school. After the war, he worked during the day and took college courses at night, studying economics. Peter met his wife, Yvonne, in England. She had also come on the Kindertransport. Both of them lost their parents and most members of their families in the Holocaust.

They decided to make a new life in America. Peter worked for the U.S. government in Washington, D.C. They have three children and three grandsons. Peter is now retired, and he and Yvonne enjoy spending time with their family and traveling.

After moving to the United States, Peter worked in the nation's capital.

A Musical Family

Four suitcases and two small violin cases were lined up in our front hall. We were ready to leave with the Kindertransport.

"Marion," Mother said quite firmly, "you have to take care of the twins and George. You are the oldest. They will listen to you."

I looked at the ten-year-old twins, dressed in identical dresses and coats. Gisi was jumping up and down with excitement while Uschi was close to tears. My brother, George, was fidgeting impatiently. Though it was still early in the morning, the taxi was already waiting to take us to the station.

I think that Mother was very brave to part with us. She had been so upset ever since our father was picked up by the Gestapo on Kristallnacht and taken to a concentration camp.

Now she was forcing a smile and telling us that she would join us soon.

On the train to Holland, Uschi clung to me, while George and Gisi looked out of the window. Uschi was always scared. Back home, Gisi had to protect her from the neighborhood bullies.

"We'll see Aunt Ruth and Uncle Walter at the boat in Holland," I tried to console her. Uschi was still worried.

"Will Mama send my cello to England?" she asked me. I assured her that she would. Uschi loved her music and was getting quite good at it. Everyone in our family was musical. I played the piano, while George and Gisi played violin. Father composed music for us to play.

We knew that there were Nazi guards on the train. Before we reached the border, they would inspect all the luggage, looking for valuables to take from us.

"Do you have anything of value?" they demanded of the frightened children. "Hey, what is in these cases?" they asked, kicking the shiny leather boxes that contained our instruments.

"Those are our violins," Gisi declared. She refused to be intimidated by the men in Nazi uniforms.

"Oh, yeah," one of them sneered. "I bet you are going to sell them for good money."

"Of course not. We play them," Gisi explained while Uschi clung to my skirt.

"Then prove it!" ordered the other man, roughly handing Gisi the instrument.

Gisi did not hesitate. She put the violin under her chin and drew the bow across the strings. The sounds of "God Save the King," Britain's **national anthem**, filled the compartment. The inspectors turned on their heels and left.

national anthem
official song of
a country

At the first station in Holland, cheerful Dutch ladies welcomed us with hot drinks and cookies. Uschi finally cheered up when she saw Aunt Ruth and Uncle Walter waiting for us at the port. "We had been hoping that your mother would let us take care of you here in Holland," they said, "but your mother is determined to send you to England."

We were able to spend a little time with our relatives before leaving on the ferry to England.

Gisi practices her violin shortly after arriving in England, 1939 (left). The Hess twins pose with their English foster parents (center). Twins Gisi and Uschi on their first day of school in Hamburg. (right).

SOUTH AMERICA

When Marion's father was taken to a concentration camp by the Nazis, her mother, Gerti, decided to send her four children to England with the Kindertransport.

After the children left, Gerti worked hard to get a visa for her husband to go to South America. He was released from the concentration camp when his visa came, but he had to leave Germany immediately. Gerti wanted to be with her four children, so she arranged to get a work permit to be a live-in maid in England.

Her job in the British household was very hard. She had to clean a big house, carry coal upstairs from the coal cellar, and tend the fires. The family she worked for would not allow Gerti's children to stay with her. They had to live with foster families, but Gerti saw them whenever possible. Gerti suffered from crippling arthritis, and she died before the family could be reunited.

Like her siblings, Gisi became a professional musician.

Like her mother, Marion also worked as a maid for a family in England. After the war, she joined her father in New York, where he had gone from South America. Marion married and raised two children. She and her husband retired to California to be close to their children.

Gisi, Uschi, and George stayed in England, and all three became professional musicians. Gisi was the first violinist in a British orchestra, Uschi played the cello in the orchestra of an opera company, and George formed his own group of string players, which gave many concerts in England. Gisi's, Uschi's, and George's children also became musicians.

Uschi poses with her cello.

ENGLAND

NEW YORK NEW YORK
UNITED STATES

Life in England

porridge
hot oatmeal

The children who arrived in England with the Kindertransport found it very hard to adjust to their new country. Aside from the loneliness of being so far from their families and friends, they had difficulty understanding what people said to them because they knew little or no English.

Above all, the weather made life very uncomfortable for the children. It is often rainy and foggy in England, and the children who arrived in the winter months suffered from the cold and damp. British homes depended on open fireplaces or small gas heaters for warmth, but these warmed only a small area. Bedrooms had no heat at all; hot water bottles were put in beds to provide a little warmth between the damp sheets.

Finally, the food in England was very different from the meals the children were used to. They longed for their mothers' cooking. The English eat **porridge** for breakfast, drink a lot of tea with milk instead of the cocoa the children remembered, and serve very thin sandwiches, not like the thick slices of rye bread that the children were used to.

Most families who took in the "refugee children," as they called them, were kind and caring. Though some of the families were Jewish, many were Christian. Almost all of the younger children were sent to local schools, but girls in their early teens often became maids or nannies for their foster parents' children. Many older boys and girls worked in factories or on farms.

Children who had no relatives or foster families to go to were given temporary shelter at a deserted summer camp called Dovercourt, not far

Some of the *Kinder* arrived in London.

from the English Channel. There they were looked after by caring people, but the weather made them miserable. Many got **chilblains**, red, itchy sores on their hands and feet. These would come back year after year.

Hitler's army marched into Poland on September 1, 1939. England had agreed to defend Poland if it was invaded, and the British government kept that promise. Two days later, on September 3, both England and France declared war on Germany.

The last of the transports reached England the day before war was declared on September 3, 1939. Almost 10,000 children from Austria, Germany, Czechoslovakia, and Poland had been taken to safety.

chilblains
red, itchy sores caused by exposure to the cold

The Brothers

LONDON
ENGLAND

"Don't be such a sissy," I told my younger brother, Stefan, who had thrown himself down on the platform and was screaming loudly. My mother and grandparents tried hard to comfort the little boy, but Stefan was only eight years old. He could not understand why he had to go to England with the Kindertransport and leave our mother and grandparents behind.

Stefan was very much a mama's boy. I was almost eleven. I knew that we were to go alone and that our mother would join us in London. Our father had died three years before.

"Sissy!" I repeated.

"I'm no sissy," Stefan protested, wiping his tears with the back of his hand. He quickly got on the train.

This class photo was taken outside a German school.

After a long journey by train and boat, we arrived in London. Our uncle and aunt met us at the station. I did not recognize them because they had left Germany a few years earlier. Unfortunately, they had no room for us in their small apartment, so they took us to a foster family. The very next day, our foster parents enrolled us in school, and we soon began to learn English.

It seemed that this couple we lived with was not used to taking care of children. They let us roam the neighborhood by ourselves. We longed to buy candy and ice cream, but we had no money, so I thought of a plan. Stefan would wait outside a tobacco shop until somebody came out with a pack of cigarettes. I told him to ask for the cards with pictures of sports heroes or famous movie stars that came in every pack. We would then sell these to our classmates.

Every Saturday morning, we also made money by helping the milkman make deliveries with his horse and wagon. He paid us ten **pence** (about 15 cents), and always gave us a free pint of **Jersey milk**. We watched Mr. Colins, our neighbor, walk down the street with his shovel to pick up the horse

pence
pennies, in British money

Jersey milk
especially rich, creamy milk from cows raised on the Isle of Jersey

manure. He used it to fertilize his garden, which produced the biggest vegetables in the neighborhood.

I tried to be a good brother to Stefan by protecting him at all times and by helping him get over his homesickness. Our mother came to London on a special visa just before the war broke out. She was a nurse and went to work in a hospital. My grandparents had to stay behind.

Along with our schoolmates, Stefan and I were **evacuated** to Oxford in order to avoid the bombing by the Germans. Working in London, Mother was not able to see us very often. We received a very good education and won **scholarships** to college.

Stefan and Ben helped the milkman with his deliveries of fresh Jersey milk.

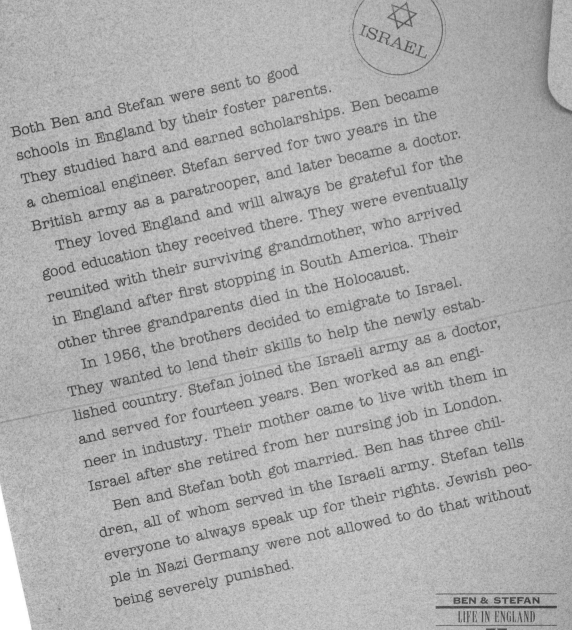

ISRAEL

Both Ben and Stefan were sent to good schools in England by their foster parents. They studied hard and earned scholarships. Ben became a chemical engineer. Stefan served for two years in the British army as a paratrooper, and later became a doctor.

They loved England and will always be grateful for the good education they received there. They were eventually reunited with their surviving grandmother, who arrived in England after first stopping in South America. Their other three grandparents died in the Holocaust.

In 1956, the brothers decided to emigrate to Israel. They wanted to lend their skills to help the newly established country. Stefan joined the Israeli army as a doctor, and served for fourteen years. Ben worked as an engineer in industry. Their mother came to live with them in Israel after she retired from her nursing job in London. Ben and Stefan both got married. Ben has three children, all of whom served in the Israeli army. Stefan tells everyone to always speak up for their rights. Jewish people in Nazi Germany were not allowed to do that without being severely punished.

Sara

A Foster Child

Children without a host family waiting for them in England went to Dovercourt Camp.

I had no relatives or foster parents to meet me when I arrived in England, so I was taken by bus with other children to Dovercourt, a summer camp which was not intended to be lived in during the winter months.

I will never forget the cold. It seemed to go right through me and chill me to the bone. No wonder the English wear woolen underwear!

The cabins we slept in were not heated. Only the recreation hall where we ate had a wood-burning stove. You had to get very close to it to feel the heat. I tried to get warm by playing ball outside with some of the other children. We had to wear all the warm clothes we had brought with us in layers,

DOVERCOURT
ENGLAND

one jacket on top of another. In the evening I was given a hot water bottle to put in my bed, but it only made a warm spot while the rest of the bed stayed cold and damp. Fortunately, a department store had donated "Wellingtons," as they called rubber boots in England, which protected our feet from the cold, rain, and snow.

Sara and her classmates pose together in Germany.

We were all waiting to be sent to English families or to a hostel or school. Every day, people came to look us over and pick out one or two children to take home. We knew these people were talking about us, but we didn't understand enough English to know what they were saying. My friend Sonya would smile and wave to the visitors, but I hid my face. Maybe I was not pretty enough to be picked.

I longed to go home to my parents, my comfortable bed, and my toys. Our apartment in Munich had been warm and cozy, and I had a big, bulky featherbed to keep me warm. I missed my parents so much. Every night I cried myself to sleep in my damp bunk bed, so quietly that no one could hear.

Eventually I was chosen by a young couple. They had no children of their own and thought that a seven-year-old girl would give them pleasure and little trouble. But I must have given them plenty of trouble.

Although Mr. and Mrs. Jones were kind to me, they did not understand me. At first, it was just a language problem. But they also did not understand what my home had been like and how I had lived in Germany.

Food was also a problem, and I didn't eat because I hated it. At home in Germany, we ate delicious, crunchy rolls with butter and jam for breakfast, but in England I was given lumpy hot porridge. I was also used to eating a hot meal at lunchtime, because everyone in my family—my father, my brother, and I—came home for lunch. I was usually starved by noon.

My English foster mother, Mrs. Jones, packed me a sandwich for lunch at school, but it wasn't enough.

Refugee children were given towels and other necessities when they arrived at Dovercourt.

I was still hungry. At five o'clock we had **high tea**, which consisted of the thinnest sandwiches I had ever seen. Some were filled with slices of "see-through" cucumber, others with some kind of fish or meat paste. I thought that they were very silly and not at all filling. Sometimes we had scones, or muffins, or baked beans on toast. Other times, Mrs. Jones offered me toast with sardines, which she called "riders on horseback." I learned to drink tea with milk in it. At home, we had tea with lemon.

Although my English soon improved, I could not explain to Mr. and Mrs. Jones how I felt. They tried to be like parents to me. I knew that they liked me, but they could not replace my parents. They never cuddled and hugged me as my father and mother had done at home.

When the war broke out, I had to leave my foster parents in London to move to the countryside.

high tea
a meal in England served late in the afternoon; it often replaces supper

Sara married and settled in England and raised a family. Although her parents, brothers, and sisters had died in the Holocaust, she never gave up looking for other members of her family who might have survived.

When her children were older, the family visited Israel. Sara checked all the lists of survivors, but she found no one. Years later, on a trip to America, she decided to look in the telephone book for people who had her family name. She called every one of them and found a woman who was married to her distant cousin. Sara was overjoyed to learn that an uncle and his family had survived and lived in Florida. Now she, her children, and her grandchildren were part of a family!

A Hard Time

My family lived in a small town not far from Frankfurt, Germany. We were the only Jews in town, and the Germans did not like us. Most of them believed Hitler when he said that the Jews were evil.

Everything bad that happened was blamed on the Jews. I felt that they blamed me personally.

FRANKFURT ■ GERMANY

My father was a butcher. After my mother died, he married again. My stepmother had two daughters. I was the youngest of the children. Father found it hard to provide for the family.

After Kristallnacht, that terrible night in November 1938, my parents and my grandfather

Ernie was just nine years old when he left for England in 1939.

were taken to a concentration camp. My grandfather returned after two days looking thin and haggard. He was forced to walk through the town wearing his tallit, and people came out and gawked at him.

As I was not allowed to attend the local German school and my parents were no longer at home, I was sent to the Jewish **orphanage** in Frankfurt. I was nine years old.

My mother's parents lived in Frankfurt, and they were forced to go to an old-age home. It was next door to the orphanage where I lived. A high fence separated the buildings. It was against the rules for the children in the orphanage to leave the building, but I longed to visit my grandparents and occasionally managed to climb the fence to see my beloved **Oma** and **Opa**.

In August 1939, just one month before war was declared, 200 children from the orphanage prepared to leave with the Kindertransport. I was lucky to be one of them. I had to say good-bye to my grandparents. I wanted to hold them and kiss them. I knew in my heart that it would be for the last time. They saw me off at the trolley car that took us to the train station. I watched as they grew smaller and smaller.

Ernie with his Oma and Opa and other relatives.

orphanage
an institutional home for children who do not have parents, or are otherwise in need

Oma
German for *Grandmother*

Opa
German for *Grandfather*

When I finally arrived in England after a long journey, I was put on a train to Glasgow, Scotland, with other children. We were told that there would be people to meet us there, but no one came. All of us were frightened. The police finally picked us up. We couldn't tell them anything because we didn't speak English. We pointed to our mouths to show them that we were hungry. The policemen gave us sandwiches and milk. Finally, someone came to take us to the youth hostel.

I didn't like it there. The beds were lumpy, and the food was terrible. I was almost happy when war broke out and I was sent to work on a farm in Dumfrieshire, not far from Glasgow.

It turned out to be an even worse place than the hostel! Although I was barely eleven years old, I had to work on the farm instead of going to school. I picked potatoes and turnips, let the horses out into the fields, fed the cows, and cleaned the stables. The farmers called me "you German," and they often hit me. The short pants I had brought with me were hardly suitable for the freezing weather and the farmwork, and I suffered from chilblains.

After the war, my parents sent for me to join them and my stepsisters in America. They had been able to emigrate shortly before war broke out.

UPDATE: Ernie

After the war, Ernie came to America, where he went to college. He settled in Philadelphia, and received a teaching degree from Temple University. He taught in the public schools for twenty years.

He loved teaching and always included what he called "The Lesson of Life." The homework assignment was: "Tell your parents, 'I love you, Mom and Dad,' and give them a kiss."

Ernie enlisted in the U.S. army during the Korean War. As he got older, Ernie suffered from a bad heart. He had to have a heart transplant, not once but twice. He devoted most of the last ten years of his life to setting up the Second Chance Group, which helps transplant patients and their families. Ernie died at the age of 66.

Ernie said that he was given three chances in life: leaving Germany, coming to America, and receiving two new hearts. His family and friends admired his courageous struggle for life. Ernie's son, Joe, said that although his Dad was not rich, he was a wealthy man because he had the love of everyone who knew him.

Ernie poses with his wife, Anne, in 1989.

UNITED
PHILA.
STATES

The War Years

CHAPTER 6

A busy London intersection, badly damaged by German bombs.

Shortly after England declared war on Germany on September 3,1939, German planes began to roar over England, dropping bombs on homes, churches, and historic buildings, damaging and destroying many of them. Life in the cities became very dangerous. Many people were injured, and others were buried under the **debris** of collapsed houses. There were big craters everywhere. It was safer to be in the country where few bombs fell.

Every night, as soon as it was dark, people in the cities had to black out all lights, so that the enemy bombers

debris
  scattered remains
  from destruction

London's children prepare for evacuation to the countryside; they carry gas masks around their necks.

air raid warden
community member
responsible for
making sure
emergency air
raid instructions
are followed

could not tell if they were flying over a city or over the countryside. People put dark cloth or black paper over their windows and doors in order to make sure that no lights showed. **Air raid wardens** who were appointed went from house to house to see that not even a crack of light was visible.

Sirens were constantly being tested; such drills had actually begun before war had even been declared, in preparation for the future. A wailing sound meant that enemy bombers were nearby. In case of an alarm, children were instructed to hide under tables and desks, or in the space under the stairs. They had to practice doing this in school.

The schools in London arranged for all children to be evacuated from the city to the countryside. Since the British feared that the Germans would use poison gas, everybody was given a gas mask, which had to be carried at all times.

The children who had come on the Kindertransport were not happy to be evacuated to the countryside. They had been in England only a short time, and had gotten used to their lives away from home. In the country, many were shifted from one household to another.

In Europe, meanwhile, Hitler's armies continued their invasion. In April 1940, they marched into Denmark and Norway. In May, Holland and Belgium were taken over, and France fell to the Germans in June. Germany had signed a **peace treaty** with the Soviet Union before war broke out, but Germany broke that treaty and invaded the Soviet Union in June 1941.

At a conference on January 20, 1942, the Nazis planned **The Final Solution**, the name they used for their plan to murder all of Europe's Jews. The Nazis rounded up the Jews in all the countries they had invaded, and took them by freight trains to concentration camps. Over six million were killed, either by the Nazi gas chambers or by the inhumane living conditions.

During the war, the British people faced difficult living conditions. Strict **rations** of food such as butter, sugar, and meat were enforced. Everyone received a single egg each week, as well as a piece of meat the size of a hamburger. They had to use dried eggs, which tasted awful.

Clothing was also rationed. Everyone received a number of stamps each month which could be used to buy shoes, underwear, stockings, dresses, pants, and shirts. To buy a coat, one had to save almost six months' worth of stamps!

In December 1941, after the Japanese attacked the U.S. naval base at Pearl Harbor, America joined Great Britain and the Soviet Union in their fight to defeat Hitler. Because these countries pledged to support one another, they became known as the **Allies**.

The Allied army, navy, and air

ration
fixed daily food allowance for each person

peace treaty
promise signed by countries pledging not to attack one another

The Final Solution
plan developed by the Nazis to kill all the Jews of Europe

Allies
countries bound by treaties to fight for, and support one another during World War II: the United States, Britain, France, and the Soviet Union

89

D-Day
June 6, 1944, the day the Allied powers invaded Europe

surrender
to give up

V-E Day
Victory in Europe Day, celebrated May 8, 1945

V-J Day
Victory over Japan Day, celebrated September 2, 1945

forces soon turned the tables on Hitler, and the war slowly came to an end. On June 6, 1944, called **D-Day**, the Allies landed in Nazi-occupied France and began to recapture Europe. On April 30, 1945, when it became clear that Germany had lost the war, Hitler killed himself in his bunker in Berlin.

Germany **surrendered** to the Allies on May 7, 1945. The war in Europe was over, and **V-E Day** was celebrated.

Japan surrendered after the United States dropped the atomic bomb on Japan, in August 1945. On September 2, 1945, **V-J Day** was declared. World War II was finally over.

Ilse

Evacuee

For three days we each carried a square cardboard box to school. There would be war, we were told, and the Germans were probably going to use poison gas, just as they had in World War I. The box, which dangled around our necks by a piece of string, contained a gas mask.

The teachers had already shown us how to put it over our faces. The smell of its black rubber was disgusting. And besides, it made you look like a pig with a long snout. Each day at school we had an air

evacuee
someone sent out of one area to the safety of another location

Ilse sits for a portrait in London after the war.

Regent Portraits Ltd.   London & Provinces

raid drill and had to wear the gas masks. We were told that when we heard the sirens, we had to get under the desks at school, or under the table or the staircase at home, until we heard the long, wailing sound of the **all-clear**.

We were evacuated from London two days before the British **Prime Minister** announced to the people over the radio that war had been declared. The large cities were in danger of being bombed, he explained, and it would be safer for the children to be in the countryside.

all-clear
siren signaling the end of an air raid drill

Prime Minister
elected leader of the British government

London schoolchildren receive gas masks in preparation for German bombing attacks.

Loaded down with knapsacks or suitcases and our gas masks, and accompanied by our teachers, we were taken by trains to an unknown destination. We looked for clues to where we were headed from the names of the stations where we stopped, but the signs were blacked out with paint. This was done so that if German paratroopers landed, they wouldn't know where they were.

After an hour's ride, we were taken off the train and loaded onto buses in groups of 30, with two teachers for each group. One of the teachers on my bus was Miss Rathbone, a small, dark-haired Welsh woman who had taught me English. She also had a lovely singing voice. I did not know the other teacher, Miss Smith. She was tall, blond, and pretty. As it turned out, she was much stricter than Miss Rathbone.

Before we got on the bus, some ladies at the station gave us each a shopping bag with a big bar of chocolate, a can of Spam (we called it "bully beef"), a can of cocoa, and other food. The bus ride lasted only half an hour—just long enough to eat the chocolate!

We stopped in front of a church, where a group of women was waiting inside. Each woman took two or three girls home with her. I didn't know any of the other children, because they had not been in my class. Because I did not have a friend to go with, I was paired off with a heavyset girl named Dorothy, who was older than I. We were sent to stay with a young widow who lived with her baby in a small cottage in the center of the village.

Mothers and foster mothers escort children to trains bound for the countryside.

It was not a happy place for me. Dorothy was a big bully. She made fun of my mistakes in English. At night, she almost pushed me out of the double bed we had to share. Finally, the widow decided she didn't want us to stay. Dorothy went home to her parents in London, despite the danger of bombings. I was sent to live with another family in the village. They were good to me, and I was happy there.

I stayed with them until I was fourteen. At that time, arrangements were made for me to live in a hostel in Birmingham, in central England.

Ilse poses with her husband, Herbert, and a friend.

SOUTH AMERICA

Ilse liked the hostel she was sent to in Birmingham. Thirty-five girls lived there, and they were like a big family. All the girls worked in factories to help out with the war effort. At a nearby hostel for boys, Ilse met Herbert who, like Ilse, had lost his parents in concentration camps. Ilse and Herbert fell in love and married.

Ilse was sure that some of her cousins had survived the Holocaust, because she knew that they had emigrated to South America before war broke out. When she and Herbert vacationed there, they tried to find her relatives. In every Latin American country they visited, they looked for their names in telephone books, and they even placed ads in the newspapers. But they could not find anyone. Could Ilse's relatives have changed their names to Spanish names?

Ilse and Herbert on their wedding day, January 2, 1944.

consul
government official appointed to represent his or her government in a foreign country

Luckily for Ilse, while at a party, she met someone from Bolivia. This was the only South American country they had not visited. Her new Bolivian friend suggested that Ilse write to the Bolivian **consul**. As it turned out, the consul found one of Ilse's long-lost cousins.

Ilse and her cousin write to each other often, and he visits Ilse and Herbert whenever he comes to America on business. Family is very important to those who have lost their loved ones in the Holocaust.

Ilse and Herbert recently celebrated their fiftieth wedding anniversary with their children and grandchildren.

Ilse and Herbert recently celebrated their 50th anniversary.

Among Strangers

I really did not want to leave London with my classmates. It had been only three months since I had arrived with the Kindertransport and Mr. and Mrs. Johnson had taken me into their home. They were kind to me and treated me as one of the family. Their daughter, Emily, was a big sister to me, and their son, Brian, had even stopped teasing me about my "funny" English. I missed my family, of course, but they had written letters assuring me that they

Trudy lived with the Ricks in this thatched-roof cottage.

would soon get their visas and come to England. We would all be together again. But when war broke out, I knew that I could not see my loved ones again until it was over.

Along with the children in my school, I was taken by train and bus to a small village in the **midlands**, about 50 miles from London. There was only one store, which also served as a post office and had the only telephone in the village. Messages were delivered on bicycle by one of the **postmistress**'s many children. On the main street there was a community building, which was the one-room schoolhouse for all the children of the village.

I was sent to stay on a small farm with two of my classmates, Joyce and Joan. Mr. and Mrs. Ricks, who asked us to call them Uncle Jim and Auntie Mary, owned the farm and had chickens and ducks, two cows, and a horse. Their two sons were in the army, so they were glad for the help we could give them on the farm.

It may be hard to believe, but there was no electricity or running water in the village. Everything had to be cooked or

midlands
  counties in the center of England

postmistress
  woman in charge of distribution of mail for her town (the masculine form is postmaster)

All the children of the one-room schoolhouse.

heated on a wood-burning stove. Drinking water was drawn from the pump, and water for washing was scooped from the rain barrel. Of course, there was no bathroom in the house. We used an **outhouse**. Can you imagine having to cross the backyard in the wintertime when you have been sitting by a blazing fire? At bedtime, we would carry a pitcher of water upstairs to the bedroom, where we three girls slept together in a double bed. On some winter mornings, the water would be frozen, and we could not get washed. In order to take a bath, we carried kettles full of hot water upstairs to fill a tub, which was just about big enough to stand in.

Joyce and Joan went back to London because they were homesick for their parents, but I had to stay. I had no parents in London to go home to, because my parents were still in Germany. But at least in the countryside I was safe from the bombs. I helped Aunt Mary with many chores. I churned butter, gathered eggs, fed the chickens, brought in firewood, and picked berries for pies.

The Ricks knew that I was Jewish. I did not accompany them to church on Sundays. I knew no Jewish people nearby, so I celebrated my holidays alone. On Yom Kippur, the holiest day of the Jewish year, I would fast, and I lit candles at Chanukah. I remembered some Jewish prayers that I had learned at home and in my Jewish school. I was sure that my parents, so far away in Germany, would be celebrating the same holidays at the same time.

outhouse
an outdoor toilet

When Christmas came, I helped Aunt Mary decorate the house, make **mince pies**, and grind the fruit for **plum pudding**. My teacher asked me to be in the Christmas play. Although I did not believe in the Christmas story, I wanted to be in the play.

I spent two happy years in the village, but left at fourteen to continue my education at a boarding school.

mince pie
  pastry filled with ground-up fruit

plum pudding
  English steamed dessert eaten at Christmastime

UPDATE: Trudy

When Trudy was fourteen, she was sent to a boarding school in the British countryside. The headmistress had brought the school to England from Germany, because she saw that Nazi Germany was not a country where children could be raised in freedom.

When Trudy arrived at the school, there were 110 students of all ages. They lived in a large mansion surrounded by many buildings which had been part of a farm, and which were now used as classrooms or as living quarters for teachers and staff. Most of the students were refugees like Trudy. Their parents were still in Nazi-occupied countries, or had emigrated to other countries. Only a few of the children had parents in England.

Trudy never saw her parents again; they died in a concentration camp. She remained in England and became a nursery school teacher. Trudy married and had a son.

The Blitz

There was a red glow in the distance. "They are bombing London again tonight," sighed Mrs. Farley. "Luckily, we are safe here." I lived with the Farleys in a small town about 50 miles north of London. I had been an evacuee for almost a year now. All the other evacuees who had come on the bus with me had already gone home to their parents, despite the danger.

My parents had escaped Nazi Germany a few months before the war and now lived in London. Because they were considered to be Germans, however, the British authorities considered them **enemy aliens**, and did not allow them to travel. They could not visit me. I begged them to let me come home, but they wouldn't let me return to London. It was safer

enemy alien
an immigrant living in a country at war with his or her native country

Ina missed her parents in London.

in the countryside now that the Germans had started bombing the large cities. In the country we had only a few stray bombs fall in the surrounding fields.

One **incendiary** came down the Farley's chimney, but it didn't explode. Air raid wardens, wearing hard hats, came right away to put out the small fire the bomb had started.

incendiary
a bomb designed to start a fire

I had come to England with the Kindertransport six months before my parents managed to emigrate from Germany. I had lived with strangers during that time, and had longed to be with my family again. My parents finally gave in and let me join them in London.

When I arrived in London, I was shocked to see that it looked very different since the last time I was there. Damage from the bombs had changed the city. There were deep craters where some buildings had stood, while other houses had no fronts or backs. You could look right into different rooms where tables, chairs, and beds were still in place. It reminded me of my dollhouse at home,

London schoolchildren carried their gas masks and emergency supplies to school with them.

A coat cost almost six months' worth of ration coupons.

the underground
name for London's subway system

where one could look into every room. Police and firemen had fenced off the bomb sites because walls could fall down at any time.

Signs with a large "S" were posted everywhere to point the way to the nearest air raid shelter. **The underground** was also a place to take shelter from bombs. When the sirens sounded a continuous rising and falling wail, it meant that enemy aircraft were on their way. Everyone headed for shelter. Not until one heard the all-clear, a long sound on one note, could one go about one's business again. This became a way of life for Londoners.

When the sirens sounded at night, people took blankets and pillows to a shelter, where mattresses were spread out. The children slept while the adults listened to the sounds of the night. A high-pitched whistle getting louder and louder meant that a bomb was coming closer. They covered their ears, waiting tensely for the explosion. If it was very loud, it had hit close by. The firing of the antiaircraft guns, or "ack-ack," as they were called because of the sound they made, went on and on. Often a plane was hit and would spiral to earth with a shrill whistle. The curious would poke their heads out of the shelter to scan the sky. The markings on the airplane's wings showed whether it was the hated **Jerry**. Everyone hoped it wasn't one of "ours" that was shot down.

As the war went on, the Germans sent the biggest and most frightening bombs, called the **doodlebugs**. They were very powerful and destructive missiles. When they flew above, one could hear their *vroom, vroom*. Even the large **barrage balloons** floating over the city were unable to stop them.

Life in London was very dangerous. Luckily, my parents and I were unharmed during the **Blitz**.

Jerry
British slang for the German forces in World War II

doodlebugs
name given to rocket-propelled missiles

barrage balloon
large balloon similar to a blimp, with wires or nets used to entangle enemy aircraft

Blitz
German for *lightning*; refers to heavy bombing attacks on British cities during World War II

Ina went to college in London and became a teacher. Her father had a small grocery store in London. With hard work and the help of his wife, he made a good living. Ina also helped them whenever she could.

Ina loved children and enjoyed teaching them. Eventually, she met a fellow teacher and they fell in love. They married and had three children.

Ina and her husband retired to a home in the countryside. Both love gardening. They grow their own vegetables, and Ina takes great pride in her beautiful flower beds. She is particularly successful with her lovely roses.

Ina and her husband have six grandchildren who love to visit their grandparents in the countryside.

After the War

Concentration camp survivors were freed by the Allies, 1945.

When V-E Day was declared on May 8, 1945, people in England celebrated in the streets. The Kindertransport children looked forward to being reunited with the families they had left behind in Nazi-occupied countries.

It took a long time for the children to learn whether their parents had survived the war years. The **Red Cross** did its best to gather all the names of those who had survived concentration camps or ghettos, as well as those who had been hidden by courageous Christians. New lists of survivors were posted every few days. Parents who knew the addresses of their children in England sent **telegrams** to let

Red Cross
international organization that helps people in need; it also arranged for prisoners of war to send postcards to their families

telegram
message sent over telegraphic wires

KRISTALLNACHT

The United States Holocaust Memorial Museum in Washington, D.C.

them know that they were alive and longing to see them again. One-third of the children who had left with the Kindertransport were reunited with at least one parent. The rest were orphans, left all alone.

Reunions with parents were not always easy or happy. More than six years had passed since the children and parents had seen one another. For the children, life in England had been very different from that of their families. They had been sheltered and fed by their British hosts, while their parents had suffered hunger, cold, and terrible cruelties. Furthermore, the children were no longer the little ones who had left home with the Kindertransport. They had grown up during their time in England, but their parents could remember their children only as the young boys and girls they had last seen and held. The survivors were about to start new lives in another country, and their children felt they had to help.

After the war, the Allies immediately set out to to find those who had

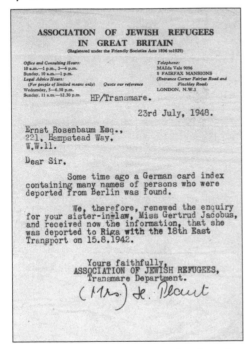

This letter confirms in 1948 the deportation of a relative to Riga in 1942.

helped Hitler and the Nazi Party to commit crimes against Jews and others. In November 1945, a special court was set up in Germany in which several Nazis who had planned and committed the cruelties against the Jews and other victims were put on trial. These trials became known as the **Nuremberg Trials**. Most of the accused were found guilty, and were either sentenced to death or sent to prison.

Some people who survived the terrible years of World War II never spoke about their experiences, while others wanted to tell all about it, however much the memory hurt. But whether or not they told about their painful past, none would ever forget it.

Nuremberg Trials
court set up to try Nazi criminals in 1945–1946

A Reunion

The war was finally over. I celebrated V-E Day with all my friends. We danced in the streets and hugged and kissed. The ugly old blackout curtains were torn from the windows, and the city was brightly lit up just like it used to be before the war.

I would soon see my family again. The last news I had received from my mother was a letter sent through the International Red Cross over three years ago. "I am well," my mother wrote, "but I miss you a lot." I wrote my answer to her on the back of the Red Cross form, which allowed a reply of only 25 words. It was very hard to tell my mother in so few words all that was in my heart. I didn't want to say that I was lonely and sad, because that would make Mother unhappy. I had to write a cheerful message.

I didn't hear from my mother again until after the war. I received a telegram from her that she would soon be coming to England.

At last, the long-awaited day came. I was very excited. I had been only nine years old when I left my home in Munich six years before. Though my father had already left for America, the German government would not let my mother and me leave. Luckily, Mother was able to send me to England with the Kindertransport a few weeks before war broke out. It was painful saying good-bye; I remember crying when I had to leave my family and friends.

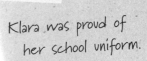

On the day I was to be reunited with my mother, I put on my school uniform with great care: a clean white blouse, the pleated gym slip tied with a braided belt, and my black felt hat with a ribbon of the school colors. When the train arrived, I tried to spot my mother. I remembered a beautiful lady, well-dressed, her dark hair curling around her face, made up with lipstick and rouge, and with large earrings dangling to her shoulders. I had always longed to be as pretty as Mother. But no one matching that description got off the train.

Klara was proud of her school uniform.

Suddenly I heard a familiar voice, and two arms were thrown around me. "Mein Klaralein (my little Klara)," the woman said. No, it couldn't be my pretty, young mother. This was a gray-haired old lady wearing a worn-out black coat. But it was my mother! She talked on and on in German about her little girl and how grown-up I was. All she wanted to do was hug and hold me, just like she used to when I was little.

After the war, many of the Kinder were left orphans.

The German language sounded strange to my ears. I never spoke it anymore. I felt very British. I called myself "Claire." Aunt Meg and Uncle Bob, my foster parents for the last five years, had been good to me. I liked my school and was proud of wearing my uniform. My schoolmates liked me. I could not imagine a different life, but Mother kept talking about joining Father in America.

Mother must have suffered terribly in Germany during the last six years. I did not ask her about it, but instead tried to make her forget all about the bad times. I knew that I had to give her all my love and take good care of her.

I would have to get used to another country and a new way of life. At least I would be with my very own family.

Klara and her mother went to live in New York with her father. Klara felt that she had to take care of her mother because she had suffered so much in a concentration camp and had still not regained her health. Klara nursed her until she died a few years later as a result of not having had regular food for three years. In the camp, she was given only watery soup and crusts of bread. On this diet, she had been forced to work in the laundry every day washing clothes for the Nazi guards.

Klara continued her schooling at City College in New York. She had always enjoyed math and science, so she decided to make it her life's work. She continued her studies in science and became a professor of biology.

Klara never married. Her father moved in with her when he became too old to take care of himself. She often visits England, and plans to live there when she retires from teaching. Klara loves her two dogs, with whom she shares her New Jersey home.

NEW YORK NEW YORK UNITED STATES

Left an Orphan

Vati
affectionate German word for *father*

C hurch bells rang, sirens wailed, there was music and dancing, and people laughed and hugged each other. The war in Europe was over!

I had not heard from my parents since they had sent me a postcard almost a year ago. Mutti had written that she was well and hoped that I was, too. She sent all her love to me and my brother, Gordon, and she prayed that we would soon be together again. She did not mention **Vati**. Was he still alive?

We waited anxiously for news about Mutti from Germany, but her name was not on the list of those who had survived. A lady who had been in the same concentration camp with her wrote to us that my mother was put on a transport to another camp a few

Anne on her first day of school in Germany, 1932.

months before the war ended. She never heard from Mutti again. Vati, she told us, had died in the concentration camp that year.

I could not cry. I had cried so many times in the past five years while I lived with strangers. Although they had treated me kindly, they were not as loving as my parents. I could not cuddle up and kiss them and share all my hurts and sadness. I kept all my feelings inside of me. Someday, I hoped to tell Mutti how I felt. Now I knew that it would never happen; I was an orphan. Luckily, I still had my brother, Gordon.

Anne's brother, Gordon, served in the British army.

Gordon was nine years older than I, and had gone to England on a student visa in the summer of 1938. When he heard about Kristallnacht, he immediately sent a telegram to my parents.

"Get Anne out of the country right away," it read. "I will find a family who can take her in."

I left with the Kindertransport four weeks later. Gordon had found work in London, where he shared a rented room with two friends not far from where I lived with an English family. I saw him every weekend. He took good care of me, but he could not replace Mutti and Vati.

As soon as the war broke out, Gordon joined the British army. I was evacuated to a tiny village in Bedfordshire and lived on a farm. Gordon was sent to France with his army unit to dig trenches for the British soldiers. Thankfully, he returned safely to England.

When I turned fourteen, my brother worried about my education. At that time, English children left school at fourteen unless they had taken exams for high school when they were eleven. I was already twelve when I came to England, so I had not taken them. Gordon found a boarding school to take me in. I was happy there and received a good education. In the meantime, Gordon fell in love and married a music teacher.

After I graduated from boarding school, I went to live with my new sister-in-law, Connie. Gordon was still in the British army and was stationed in Ireland. He came home whenever he had leave. I had hoped that Connie would be a big sister to me, but we did not get along. I went to work in the public library and took college classes in the evenings to become a librarian.

Anne and her classmates pose in their handmade hats and scarves, 1936.

I met many people at the library. One day, a handsome American soldier came in and asked for a book. He told me that he had spent the last few years in Europe and was now waiting for his turn to go home. His name was Frank and he was from Philadelphia. We began to spend a lot of time together and soon fell in love. We were married three months later.

Frank left for home while I waited for the American government to provide a ship to take me and other "war brides" to America. Four months later, I was reunited with my new husband in America.

UNITED
PHILA.
STATES

Anne and Frank settled in Philadelphia and have lived there since 1946. They moved in with Frank's mother and sister until they found an apartment of their own. There was a shortage of housing at that time because of all the soldiers returning home.

Anne worked as a librarian at the Philadelphia Free Library until the birth of her son. Two years later, she and Frank had a daughter. As a veteran, Frank was given money from the government to continue his college classes, which the war had interrupted. After college, he taught in public school while he continued his studies for a doctorate. He eventually became a professor of history at a university.

A few years ago, Anne and Frank celebrated their fiftieth wedding anniversary. They are retired now and spend a lot of time writing; both of them have had their work published. They make time, though, for their four granddaughters.

Anne and her husband, Frank, recently celebrated their fiftieth anniversary.

A Happy Ending

munitions
weapons

During the war, I worked in an English **munitions** factory that made bomb parts. I could not sleep at night, because in my dreams I saw the bombs I had helped to make exploding in the middle of a street in Hamburg. My mother was walking on one side of the street and my father on the other side. When the war finally ended, so did my nightmares.

I knew that my father had died in the Holocaust, but I had received no news of my mother. I had a feeling that she was still alive. The rest of my family was scattered all over the world, and I didn't know where to look for them. They did not seek me out, and I couldn't remember their names.

I was only ten years old when our family broke up. My father was Jewish, and my mother converted to Judaism. However, under Hitler's laws she was considered Christian. Although they loved each other, my parents divorced, thinking that would be the best way to protect my brother and me from the Nazi terrors. Because Mother wanted her children to have a Jewish education, I was sent to live in an orphanage in Hamburg, the closest big city to have a Jewish school. I hated the orphanage and was glad to leave with the Kindertransport to England.

Celia (left) and friends in Hamburg, 1938, shortly before she left for England.

After I was evacuated to the countryside, I got very little schooling. I wanted to go to work, so I moved into a hostel with other girls. When I was old enough, I went to work in a munitions factory. One day, a friend told me that she knew a British soldier, Ken, who was stationed near Hamburg. She told him about my mother, who was still living there. Ken visited my mother, and she gave him my picture. I met Ken when he returned to England on leave. He was surprised that I was an adult, for he had expected to see the young child from the photograph.

Ken and I started to see each other more often. He was the first person I ever met to whom I could tell my innermost feelings. We fell in love and got married. A year later, we had a daughter. I was very anxious to return to Germany to see my mother, but we did not have the money. I tried to borrow the money, but without success. It took another year before I could take the baby to Hamburg to meet her grandmother.

I think of myself as English and Jewish. When Ken and I visited Israel, we went to **Yad Vashem**, the memorial to the Jews who perished in the Holocaust. While there, I felt very close to my father and my own Jewishness, and I cried. From that day on, I felt more at peace with myself.

Yad Vashem
memorial built in Jerusalem to remember all who died in the Holocaust

Israel's Holocaust memorial museum, Yad Vashem.

Celia and Ken live in England. They raised two children, one of whom moved to Australia.

Celia's mother continued to live in Germany after the war, until she died in 1996 at the age of 98. Despite the miles between them, Celia had visited her mother as often as she was able.

When Celia was in Israel, she donated the money she had inherited from her father to an Israeli orphanage. She remembered the unhappy time she had spent many years earlier at the orphanage in Hamburg, and she hoped her donation would help to make life more pleasant for the children of the Israeli children's home.

What has she learned in her life? "Live today, and share your feelings. Be yourself." Celia expresses her feelings and thoughts by writing poetry. Doing so helps her cope with her loneliness since Ken's death.

Celia and Ken on a visit to Australia, 1991.

ENGLAND

Many Countries Many Homes

guardian
  person responsible
  for taking care of
  another person

chaplain
  clergyman in
  the military

I lived in many different foster homes in England; some good and some not so good. During the last years of the war, I stayed in a hostel with other girls. As soon as the war ended, however, I was able to return to London to stay with my **guardians**. The hostel I had lived in was preparing to house orphans who had survived the Holocaust.

My sister, Ruth, and I had not heard from our parents for two years. Then one day my guardians received a telegram from Italy. It was from a Jewish **chaplain**, Captain Rappaport, in the American army. He asked if my foster parents knew two girls named Ruth and Lilly. We didn't know what it meant, but we felt that it had something to do with our parents. My guardians cabled back, saying they knew the girls, and that they were both well.

It turned out that the chaplain had met my parents in southern Italy, where my father was working as an **interpreter** for the Americans. I later learned what had happened to my parents.

My father had escaped from Vienna by crossing the Austrian border into Yugoslavia. Six months later, he sent a guide to bring my mother illegally across the border. Together, my parents traveled through Yugoslavia, barely staying ahead of the Germans. They crossed into northern Italy and made their way south, where they met up with the American army. Since my father spoke English and Italian, he was given a job as an interpreter.

My sister took me to Italy to reunite with our parents. I really did not want to go there to live with them. They were like strangers to me; I could not remember them. I had forgotten how to speak German. I had become accustomed to my life in England, and the idea of living in another country frightened me. I had always been a shy child. I did not want to go to a new school or have to learn Italian.

interpreter
one who translates conversation between people who speak different languages, allowing them to communicate with each other

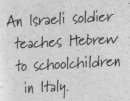
An Israeli soldier teaches Hebrew to schoolchildren in Italy.

It was very difficult living with my parents again. My mother knew no English, and my older sister had to translate for me. My father treated me like a six-year-old because in his mind he had his little girl back. He did not realize that I had grown up in the years I had lived in England.

I learned a little Italian from a neighbor who gave me lessons. I went to school, but it was very different from the English schools. The children in my class were not all the same age. Most of them had received no schooling during the war. There were also many children of returning soldiers. I just wanted to be as small as possible, so I would not be noticed. Even now, I often wish I were a "gray lady." I wanted to be just gray; not white, not black, just nothing.

My guardians in England helped our family to emigrate to England after living a year and a half in Italy. They even arranged for working papers for my father, but he could only get a **menial** job.

After almost a year in England, our family emigrated to Israel. It was yet another move for me, and I had to learn still another language.

menial
low-paid labor

Like many *Kinder* and other Holocaust survivors, Lilly eventually settled in Israel.

Lilly stayed in Israel. She served in the Israeli army and later became a kindergarten teacher. Her secret dream had always been to become a singer, but there was no money for her musical training. She took care of both her parents until they died.

In 1976, Lilly went back to Vienna, her hometown. She wanted to find the house she had lived in as a little girl, but she did not feel comfortable there. It was no longer home. Lilly went back to Israel feeling that there was no other country to go back to—neither Austria nor England nor Italy. She settled in Jerusalem and is happy there.

Epilogue

The *Kinder* are getting old now. Most of them are grandfathers and grandmothers. They have never forgotten their homes in Europe and the unselfish parents who sent them to England to safety. It was very hard for the families to part. The parents hoped and prayed that their children would be taken care of in a strange country. Most of them were treated kindly by their British foster parents, even if they had to do the household chores or take care of younger children; others were treated like servants.

The *Kinder* did not always feel a part of the families that had taken them in. They were lonely, and they missed the love and affection of their own homes. Sometimes they would cry when they were alone, but more often they bravely tried to hide their unhappiness. After all, they were grateful to England for saving them from the fate that 1.5 million children suffered in the Holocaust. They ate the unfamiliar food without complaint and learned to speak a strange new language.

Former classmates and *Kinder*, Lou, Irene, Celia, and Eva share memories at a Kindertransport reunion in 1994.

Six long years went by, and the *Kinder* adapted to their lives in England. They went to school and studied hard. During this time, they heard very rarely from their loved ones, if at all. Although they never lost the hope of seeing them again once the war was over, many of them were not so lucky.

Most of the *Kinder* were left orphans and had to find the strength to make it on their own. It was not easy. Many studied to become doctors, nurses, teachers, or social workers, in order to be helpful to others. They married, had children, and created loving homes, just like the ones they remembered. They tried to grow up the way their parents would have wanted them to, as good citizens and helpful to those in need.

In 1989, there was a reunion in London, and 1,000 of the 10,000 *Kinder* attended. They came from all corners of the world, hoping to meet old friends from the same town, school, hostel, or boarding house. People who had not seen one another for 50 years were reunited. They hugged and kissed and talked about their lives.

The following year, the *Kinder* who lived in the United States organized an American group. Some 500 attended their reunion. In small groups, the *Kinder* talked about their experiences of coming to America from England and raising a family in a free country. The love and protection they remembered from their own homes, they passed on to their children. In the past, they had often hesitated to talk about growing up alone in England among strangers, so as not to upset their own children. Now they could talk freely to other *Kinder*.

What have the *Kinder* learned from their experiences?

- To be thankful for being saved from the Holocaust
- To remember the kindness of strangers
- To tell their stories to others
- To help children in need, whoever they are, whatever their nationality, color, or religion
- To appreciate people's differences

Anne and Eva